MIND VS. MUSCLE

THE PSYCHOLOGY OF SPORTS

SOCCER

CATHLEEN SMALL

Gareth Stevens
PUBLISHING

Please visit our website, **www.garethstevens.com**.
For a free color catalog of all our high-quality books,
call toll free 1-800-542-2595 of fax 1-877-542-2596.

Cataloging-in-Publication Data

Names: Small, Cathleen.
Title: Soccer / Cathleen Small.
Description: New York : Gareth Stevens Publishing, 2019. | Series: Mind vs muscle: the psychology of sports | Includes glossary and index.
Identifiers: LCCN ISBN 9781538225387 (pbk.) | ISBN 9781538225462 (library bound)
Subjects: LCSH: Soccer--Juvenile literature.
Classification: LCC GV943.25 S63 2019 | DDC 796.334--dc23

First Edition

Published in 2019 by
Gareth Stevens Publishing
111 East 14th Street, Suite 349
New York, NY 10003

© 2019 Gareth Stevens Publishing

Produced for Gareth Stevens by Calcium Creative Ltd
Editors: Sarah Eason and Jennifer Sanderson
Designers: Paul Myerscough and Simon Borrough
Picture researcher: Rachel Blount

Picture credits: Cover: Shutterstock: Natursports; Inside: Shutterstock: AGIF: p. 20; Artnana: p. 15; Aspen Photo: pp. 1, 22; Paolo Bona: p. 14b; CHEN WS: pp. 30-31; Daykung: p. 37t; Dslaven: p. 10t; Dziurek: p. 19; Juergen Faelchle: p. 9; Frank Gaertne: p. 32; Mai Groves: p. 31r; Mitch Gunn: p. 28; Stefan Holm: p. 29; Katatonia82: pp. 10b, 43; Andrii Kobryn: p. 41; Herbert Kratky: pp. 12, 33; Liukov: pp. 6, 7; Makieni: p. 27; Maxisport: pp. 24, 35, 38; Monkey Business Images: pp. 18, 34; Muzsy: p. 11; Natursports: p. 39; Jakkrit Orrasri: pp. 23, 5t; Photo Works: p. 44; A.Ricardo: pp. 36-37b; Rnoid: p. 5b; Antonio Scorza: p. 42; Sirtravelalot: p. 45; TandemBranding: p. 40; Ververidis Vasilis: p. 26; Vlad1988: p. 25; Wavebreakmedia: p. 4; Wonlopcolors: p. 13; Marcos Mesa Sam Wordley: p. 21; Wikimedia Commons: Adrian Roebuck: p. 14t; Noah Salzman: p. 17; Scanpix: p. 16; Fanny Schertzer: p. 8.

Printed in the United States of America

CPSIA compliance information: Batch #CS18GS:
For further information contact Gareth Stevens, New York, New York, at 1-800-542-2595.

CONTENTS

CHAPTER 1

THE PSYCHOLOGY OF
Sports

Anyone can play sports. All it takes is the willingness to learn the basic rules of the game and give it a try. To play sports well, though, people need some level of **athleticism**. And to be excellent at sports, players need not only athletic skill but also a deeper understanding of the **strategy** behind the game. In any sport, the strongest athletes have a combination of physical skills and the mental aptitude to understand how to play the game in the best possible way.

WHAT IS PSYCHOLOGY?

Psychologists provide people with tools to help them better understand themselves and learn how to cope with stress and frustration. A psychologist provides a second set of eyes for any situation a person is struggling with. For example, if a student is struggling with extreme anxiety over taking tests, a psychologist can help them understand why they feel anxious and teach them how to manage that stress.

Soccer players have to keep their mind on the game if they want to play well.

The same is true in sports psychology. Sports psychologists are trained to help athletes look at their game play and understand more about how to improve on their weaknesses and make the most of their strengths. Sports psychologists can teach players tools to help battle anxiety on the playing field, court, pool, or wherever their sport is played. In sports, the name of the game is to be the best you can be. To encourage players to reach their potential, coaches and players often turn to sports psychology. Sports psychology looks at how psychology affects sports performance and how participating in sports affects an athlete's **mental state**.

Physical preparation before the game is half the battle. The other half is mental preparation.

Fancy footwork can help a player be formidable on the field, but focus is essential to using that power.

Sports psychology techniques, such as **goal setting** and **self-talk**, can help players improve their performance. They can also encourage team **unity**. Sports psychologists work with coaches and players to determine the techniques that will best benefit the team and enable its individual players to succeed. By following their psychologist's advice, players can perfect the combination of athleticism and **mental agility** that is necessary to be truly great soccer players.

NEUROSCIENCE MEETS PSYCHOLOGY

MIND vs. MUSCLE

Sports psychology works with science to develop techniques to help athletes maximize performance. Soccer players are under particular pressure because throughout the world, soccer is incredibly popular—soccer players at the highest levels of competition may be playing in front of more than 40,000 spectators at a time, and that does not even include the viewers watching the game on television or other electronic devices. Playing in such a bright spotlight can be incredibly difficult.

Sports psychologists have learned through developments in **neuroscience** that the key to top performance lies in the prefrontal lobe of the brain. That part of the brain is vital to decision-making, awareness, and anticipation—all skills that are crucial for playing soccer. With this in mind, sports psychologists have developed techniques, such as positive self-talk and anger management strategies, that help players keep the prefrontal lobe of their brain from becoming overloaded.

Sports psychologists help athletes deal with the distractions of cheering and chanting fans.

Confidence breeds success! Players engage in confidence-building activities before stepping onto the field.

PSYCHOLOGY IN SOCCER

Mental strategy is important in individual sports, such as swimming and tennis, but it is equally important in team sports, such as soccer. In a team sport, players must aim to always play their own personal best, but they must try to help the team as a whole play its best, too.

Interestingly, though, the soccer world has been slower to adopt sports psychology than some other sports. Performance coach Tom Bates thinks it is because the word "psychology" has a negative association for some players and coaches. He mentioned meeting a prominent soccer club captain, who announced that Bates must be "the new shrink" who had come to wave something in front of his face. This was a reference to the stereotypical idea of hypnotism, where a hypnotist swings a watch on a pendulum in front of a patient's face to put them in a relaxed state. Bates assured the captain that he was mistaken—that Bates was there simply to help the players better their performance.

Performance psychologist Barry Cripps feels similarly to Bates and suggested that there is a **stigma** associated with psychologists in the soccer world. Players fear that if the greater soccer community finds out they use a psychologist, they will not be given a spot at a soccer club.

Both Bates and Cripps, though, believe that the importance of sports psychologists to soccer clubs cannot be ignored. Stories of soccer players whose games have suffered when they have gone through personal difficulty or trauma seem to support that view. For example, Wilson Palacios, a celebrated midfielder, saw his game suffer noticeably after his brother was kidnapped and killed. Angel Di Maria, also a strong player, was a burglary victim, and his play deteriorated after the event.

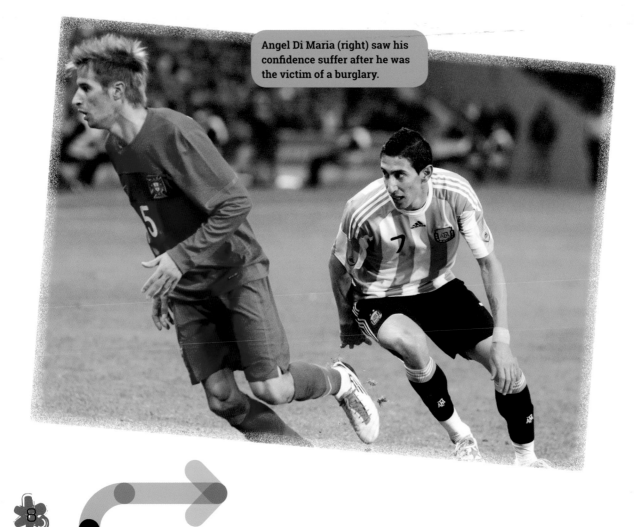

Angel Di Maria (right) saw his confidence suffer after he was the victim of a burglary.

IN THE GAME

A player does not necessarily need to suffer trauma to have it affect their play, though. Any distraction that takes the player's mind away from the game can negatively affect play, even if it is a simple, quick distraction. Even for players who do not think they have distractions, sports psychology can help them go that extra mile to make sure their brain is 100 percent on the game.

Soccer players have a lot to focus on. In theory, a soccer player's focus is always on the ball. The player is either attacking, trying to get the ball and move it down the field on offense, or trying to keep the ball from getting too close to the goal on defense. But a player's focus also must be on what their teammates are doing at any given time. One key to a successful soccer game is to keep the team spread out across the field to make sure the field is well covered, so players have to watch where their teammates are and plan the best possible position on the field based on that. It is a lot to keep in mind at once, and any distraction, no matter how small, can prevent a player from managing all these details as effectively as possible.

CHAPTER 2

THE BASICS OF
Soccer

In parts of the world other than the United States, soccer is called association football, or just football. It makes sense, because soccer is a game played mostly with the feet. However, in the United States, there is already a game called football, so what the rest of the world knows as "football" is called "soccer."

THE LOCATION

Soccer is played on a field, which can be referred to as the pitch. The field may be in a stadium, as is the case for professional games, or it may just be at a school or in a park. Soccer fields are pretty simple. There is a goal at each end that normally has a net in it. However, soccer can easily be played without the net—it just means that the goalkeeper will have to run to fetch any ball that gets through the goal.

> Soccer can be played anywhere, from a street to a field in a stadium filled with thousands of fans.

Most soccer fields follow **FIFA** standards: They are between 100 yards (90 m) and 130 yards (120 m) long and 50 yards (45 m) to 100 yards (90 m) wide. They usually have real grass on them, as opposed to artificial turf, because it has been found that more injuries happen on artificial turf.

There is also a variety known as indoor soccer, which is played in an indoor area, sometimes with fewer than the usual 11 on a team. Indoor soccer is not nearly as popular as outdoor soccer, but there are still leagues worldwide devoted to it.

Indoor soccer may not be popular as outdoor soccer, but it's still played in many areas.

THE EQUIPMENT

There is not a lot of equipment required for soccer. Although the net for the goal is not required, it is nearly always used in official games. Regulation soccer balls are generally designated as size 5, and they are just over 8.5 inches (22 cm) in diameter. They weigh between 14 ounces (397 g) and 16 ounces (454 g). These balls consist of a latex **bladder** covered in hexagonal panels that are stitched together to form the distinctive pattern of a soccer ball.

Soccer uniforms consist of a shirt, shorts, shin guards, and cleats.

The standard uniform, or strip, consists of a shirt, shorts, socks, shin guards, and cleats. Shin guards are worn underneath or on top of socks, over the players' shins, to protect them from kicks to the shin that inevitably occur when an opposing player is attempting to kick the ball. Cleats are shoes that have studs on the bottom to help grip the grass. The studs are made of plastic, rubber, or metal. When soccer is played on artificial turf, cleats are not worn. This may explain why more injuries tend to occur on artificial turf. In addition to this gear, goalkeepers usually wear special gloves to help grip the ball.

THE POSITIONS

There are 11 players from each team on the soccer field at any given time. Position names sometimes vary slightly depending on the league, but they are generally the same.

In a soccer match, there is always one goalkeeper, or goalie, for each team on the field. The goalkeeper protects the goal—they are the last line of defense for the team. If the goalkeeper fails to stop the ball from going through the goal, then the opposing team gains a point.

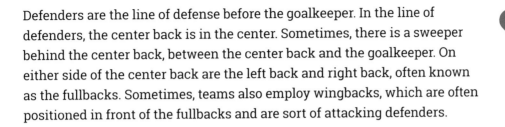

Defenders are the line of defense before the goalkeeper. In the line of defenders, the center back is in the center. Sometimes, there is a sweeper behind the center back, between the center back and the goalkeeper. On either side of the center back are the left back and right back, often known as the fullbacks. Sometimes, teams also employ wingbacks, which are often positioned in front of the fullbacks and are sort of attacking defenders.

The offensive players are often called forwards. They are positioned closer than any other player to the opposing team's goal. They are the players who take an offensive strategy, trying to score on the opposing team's goals. Forwards may play defense occasionally as needed, but mostly, they are offensive players. The forward positions are generally named center forward (sometimes called the striker), second striker, and wingers. Wingers typically play toward the edges, on the wings of the field.

Midfielders play around the center of the field, between the defenders and the forwards. They play both defense and offense—they try to capture the ball from the opposing team and feed it ahead to the forwards, who can then go attempt to score on the opponent's goal. Midfielders consist of center midfield, defensive midfield, attacking midfield, and wide midfield.

A typical soccer lineup includes a goalie, defenders, midfielders, and forwards.

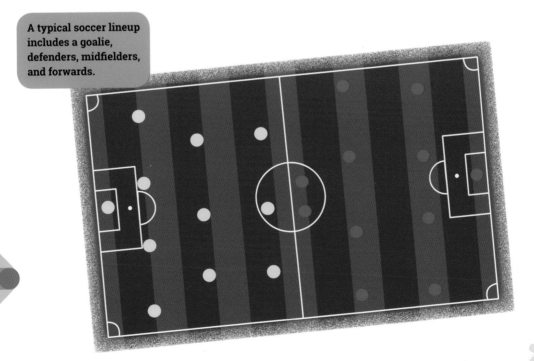

EARLY SOCCER STRATEGIES

Soccer officially began in England, in the United Kingdom, in 1863, but it is thought that the ancient Chinese played a form of the game in the third century BC. Some versions of the game were also played in **Medieval Europe**, but the game as we know it today came from England in 1863.

When soccer was first played in England, players did not have specific positions. The ball was kicked as hard and as long as possible, and players ran toward it. The aim was to get the ball in the goal, just as it is today, but many of the formal rules were not yet created. To get the ball in the goal, players mostly just dribbled down the field as far as they could and then kicked the ball as hard as they could toward the goal. Players did not often pass the ball, which is very different from soccer today, where strategy is a huge part of the game.

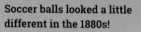

Soccer balls looked a little different in the 1880s!

Some rules in soccer, such as the offside rule, came into being long after the game was first played.

In 1863, the year thought to be the start of formal soccer, the **offside rule** was created. A player is offside if they are closer to the opponent's goal than both the ball and a defender other than the goalkeeper. In other words, a player from the **offensive team** cannot wait right next to the opposing team's goal for a ball to be passed. The player needs to remain behind the ball and behind at least one of the other team's defenders.

Very early soccer strategy in the 1860s and 1870s used a 1-2-7 formation, with one center back, two halfbacks, and seven forwards. Center backs are defenders, and halfbacks can play offense or defense. Forwards are offensive players. This early strategy emphasized offense and left defense somewhat thin.

By the 1880s, soccer teams had realized that the offense-heavy dribbling strategy of the 1-2-7 formation was not the most effective. So, they switched to a 2-3-5 pyramid formation, with two center backs, three halfbacks, and five forwards. Since the team members were more spread across the field, this strategy emphasized passing and moved away from the dribble-heavy strategy of the early days of soccer. Passing strategy is still heavily used in soccer today.

Soccer was played in Europe and the Soviet Union long before it was commonly played in the United States.

MOVING TO MODERN SOCCER STRATEGIES

Popular soccer formations changed throughout the early 1900s. The overall game strategy began to shift from an offense-heavy strategy to a more balanced strategy of offense and defense. In the late 1950s, the 4-2-4 formation became popular. It is thought to be the **predecessor** of the soccer formations used today. In the 4-2-4, the team uses four fullbacks (defensive players), two halfbacks, and four forwards (offensive players). In this formation, there is thinner coverage in the middle of the field, so the fullbacks take a much greater role in protecting the goal. The general defensive strategy is for the fullbacks to intercept the ball from the other team's offense and then quickly pass it up the field to their own offense, who can take it to the goal. Brazil used this formation to win the 1958 World Cup, and since then, variations of it have been used in modern soccer.

Brazil's Pelé (right) fights for the ball against Swedish goalkeeper Kalle Svensson in the 1958 World Cup Final.

ALL IN THE MIND

Abby Wambach and Motivation

One branch of sports psychology looks at **motivation**. Athletes can be motivated **intrinsically**, by factors inside themselves, or **extrinsically**, by external factors such as money or fame. Abby Wambach, a forward on the U.S. women's national soccer team before her retirement, is a two-time Olympic gold medalist and a FIFA Women's World Cup champion. She also won the U.S. Soccer Athlete of the Year award six times and is one of the world's top international goal scorers.

Wambach spoke about how identifying her motivation was important in helping her decide to continue playing soccer. As a young player, she knew she had a lot of potential, but she knew she had to work hard to make it come to something. And she questioned what exactly was motivating her: Was she doing it for her family or for other people? Or was she doing it for herself?

Ultimately, Wambach decided she was doing it for herself—she identified her motivation as internal. From that point on, she realized that she was the person who had to constantly motivate herself to push harder and play better every day. Motivation happens on a continuum, she says—and you have to continually motivate yourself to play better.

Abby Wambach saw her game improve when she identified what motivated her to play—which was herself.

CHAPTER 3

COACHING AND TEAM
Strategies

A good soccer coach knows that the best way to have a winning team is to make sure that the team members are all working well together and playing to their best ability individually. To do this, the coach may use numerous sports psychology techniques.

MENTAL IMAGERY

In a sense, mental imagery is using pictures rather than movements to practice a skill. Instead of doing a goal-shooting **drill**, the coach might have players envision shooting the ball into the goal in various scenarios. Bill Beswick, a sports psychologist for many English soccer teams, including Manchester United, says that mental imagery has several benefits for players and coaches:

- It allows players to see themselves as winners.
- It reinforces players' beliefs in themselves.
- It teaches players strategies to cope with situations that may come up on the field.

Coaches work hard with their players to build overall team strategies.

- It lets players practice mentally what they will experience on the field.
- It helps players learn to focus and to ignore distractions.
- It helps players improve their relaxation, so that they can use the right level of energy out on the field.

When players use mental imagery, they may use **external imagery**, where they see themselves as if they were watching a movie, or **internal imagery**, where they see the images as if they are doing the activity. Either type of imagery will work. Internal imagery gives the player a more realistic sense of actually performing the actions. External imagery is equally useful because it helps players "see" themselves playing well.

MOTIVATION

If a team loses motivation, it is not likely to be a winning team. Similarly, a player who has lost motivation will not play to their best ability. So, when a coach senses players or the team as a whole losing motivation, they can use sports psychology techniques to motivate the team.

One way to motivate the team is to make sure the practices are mentally and physically interesting. Doing the same drills, or exercises, over and over is boring for players, both mentally and physically. Mixing up the drills with some new ones can keep players more interested and motivated.

Motivation is important to a winning soccer team.

GOAL SETTING

Goal setting is another sports psychology technique that coaches can use to motivate players. If a team is doing really poorly overall, it may be hard for the players to see anything positive to work toward. By setting small, manageable goals that the team can actually meet, coaches can let team members see their progress and keep them motivated to reach for the next goal.

Coaches also keep in mind that setting goals too high can backfire. If a team is at the bottom of the league, it is unrealistic to expect that the team will win the league championship. Players may become disheartened if their coach pushes them to meet a goal they have very little hope of achieving. However, coaches can set smaller, more achievable goals to keep players motivated to improve.

SELF-CONFIDENCE

Players without confidence will not perform well. Coaches are constantly working to make sure that players are confident in their skills—but not so confident that they become **cocky** and start taking risks on the field.

Smart coaches instill self-confidence in their players and help them set goals to keep them moving forward.

Some coaches use the simple technique of positive reinforcement. They praise players for what they do well to build up their confidence. Some encourage positive self-talk, in which players may recite daily affirmations that will ultimately improve their view of themselves. Others have team members study the play of soccer legends and emphasize what those players did well. Some turn negatives into positives: If a player is afraid of failing at something on the field, the coach will encourage them to look on it as a challenge. Instead of saying, "I can't," they will encourage the player to say, "I'm up for the challenge."

Confidence can make the difference between a good player and a great one, like Cristiano Ronaldo.

MIND vs. MUSCLE

CRISTIANO RONALDO: THE POWER OF CONFIDENCE

Cristiano Ronaldo, a forward who plays for Spanish club Real Madrid and the Portuguese national team, is one of the best soccer players of all time. Like all great players, Ronaldo has incredible athletic skill. More than that, though, he has **mental strength**. Sir Alex Ferguson, who managed Ronaldo when he played for Premier League team Manchester United, called Ronaldo one of the most courageous players he had ever seen. While most players pass the ball often, Ronaldo has the confidence in himself and the mental courage to drive right into the defense with the ball. Ferguson thinks that Ronaldo's belief in himself is what makes him succeed often in this high-risk strategy.

CHAPTER 4

OFFENSIVE Strategies

There are two main objectives in soccer. The first is scoring as many goals as possible. The second is keeping the opposing team from scoring goals. One of the simplest but most important offensive strategies in soccer is to keep the ball moving at all times. If the ball is not moving, it is much easier for the opposing team to steal it. The ball moves fast in soccer, so if the team keeps the ball moving, the opposing team constantly has to track where the ball is going and may have to change its strategy to try to steal the ball and prevent a goal.

PASSING

Players can move the ball by dribbling and passing. If one player dribbles the ball down the field, numerous players from the opposing team can try to steal the ball from that one player.

In soccer, the basic aim is to move the ball forward to score goals.

However, if the ball is constantly being passed between team members, the opposing team has much more ground to defend and is much less likely to take control of the ball.

Passing is exhausting for the opposing team. If a team is constantly passing the ball, the opposing team will have to constantly change course in pursuit of the ball, which is tiring. A team that passes well will tire out the opposition— making it a wise strategy.

Passing not only conserves energy for players, but it also exhausts the opposing team.

For the team with the ball, passing takes much less energy than dribbling. Offensive teams that pass the ball a lot conserve, or save, their energy, and at the same time tire out the defense who is trying to keep up with the constantly moving ball.

Even when a player does not have the ball, they should always be moving. A player who has just passed the ball to someone else can then position themselves in an open spot closer to the goal. Soccer is a fast-paced game in which the players are always moving.

ALL IN THE MIND

Lionel Messi: Multitasker

Many people consider Lionel Messi one of the best players the sport of soccer has ever seen. Messi is a forward for Spanish club FC Barcelona and plays in the Argentinean national soccer team. One of his greatest strengths is his flexibility—he succeeds in nearly every position on the field. Pep Guardiola, who at one time managed FC Barcelona, said that Messi would play well in any position but is ultimately the best defender in the world. In other words, no matter where you put Messi, he plays well.

Messi's ability to play well in any position is partly due to athletic skill, but it is also due to his understanding of soccer strategy. He is always studying the teams and the game, then readjusting his position and strategy based on what he sees.

Lionel Messi is thought to be one of the greatest soccer players of all time.

Players learn passing through drills. Just like in any sport, drills are important for building muscle memory and improving athletic skills. However, players can also use mental imagery to help them learn better passing skills. Players who can visualize where the ball will go when they pass it, will be able to execute the pass a split second quicker than players who have to stop and think about where to pass. In a fast-paced game like soccer, a split second is everything.

Having players imagine themselves passing the ball to each other as they move down the field can improve their confidence, too. Players who visualize themselves successfully passing the ball to teammates build much-needed confidence in their passing abilities. It is a bit like a visual affirmation—if players see themselves doing something well often enough, they will begin to believe it.

Goal setting can be useful here, too. If a team is performing poorly in part because players tend to "hog" the ball and not pass it to their teammates, the coach can set goals such as passing the ball to another player every five seconds. If players work to meet those goals, passing will soon become a natural routine to them.

Players can use passing drills and mental imagery to improve their game.

DRIBBLING

Although passing is an incredibly important skill, dribbling is important, too. Dribbling is when a player moves a ball down the field using his or her feet. Usually, this is accomplished by tapping the ball lightly as one runs down the field, pushing it slightly ahead. These taps are lighter than full kicks—a full kick would move the ball too far ahead of the player, which would create an opportunity for the opposition to steal the ball. Dribbling is designed to keep the ball moving in front of the player but very close to their feet.

Although it might seem difficult to think about, one key to successful dribbling is not looking at the ball. Players need to keep their eyes ahead and on the field to watch for opposing players trying to steal the ball. They also need to look for teammates to whom they might pass the ball, in order to move it farther down the field. Players who look down at the ball will miss all the other play activity, and keeping the whole game in mind is critical to soccer success. Also, of course, players who look down run the risk of slamming straight into a player directly in front of them!

The feet do the work in dribbling—the eyes focus on what is ahead.

For soccer players, the footwork becomes second nature.

Just like passing, dribbling is learned by drills and practice. Strong dribblers use both feet (even though many favor one foot over the other), and they generally use the inside of their feet to keep the best control of the ball. It is not a difficult skill once it is mastered, but it does require some **dexterity**.

Dribblers also need to be able to change direction quickly, which requires skill. Players use a number of techniques to effectively dribble the ball, including a scissors move, which unbalances and confuses the opponent, and a shielding move, where the player uses their body to block the opponent from the ball.

In all cases, visualization can help. If a player can visualize effectively dribbling the ball and moving it down the field while protecting it from the opposing team, they will be able to use that visualization to move the ball while keeping their eyes on the field, rather than looking down at their feet.

PATH OF MOVEMENT

Whether players are dribbling or passing, the way in which they move on the field can provide an effective offensive strategy. For example, it is a natural tendency to run straight toward the goal that the player is attempting to score. However, that is a very predictable path—straight down the field toward the goal. Defenders can easily see what an offensive player is doing and position themselves appropriately to intercept the ball.

If, instead, the offensive players run diagonally, it is much harder for defenders to protect their goal effectively. There are holes between the defensive players on a team—usually, there is one in the center and one on each side of the field, both near the goal and closer to midfield. Between the defenders are holes, and if the offensive players can run diagonally and zigzag through the holes, it can make it much harder for the defenders to effectively block the offense's movement.

It is not enough to run across the field; players need to try to distract the defense to make it past them.

Players must quickly assess the pitch to figure out where defenders are before making a pass or a strike.

Similarly, if the offensive players can pass to players from sideline to sideline, it can be confusing and tiring for the defense, as they are trying to track the ball as it crisscrosses the field.

There is also a strategy where players on a team overlap their runs to give the player with the ball more space. For example, if a striker is taking a ball up the sideline, a fullback can run up and pass the striker. This then pushes back the defensive player and gives the striker more room to move and/or an opening to make a pass.

Sometimes, a team will use a long-ball strategy to move the ball. In this strategy, a defender will kick the ball in a long pass, far up the field, to the striker or other forward. Meanwhile, the other offensive players on that team look for open spaces, because the opposing team will see the long pass coming toward the striker or forward and quickly move to cover that player. The striker or forward will have only a split second to pass the ball off to another player before the other team's defense converges on them.

CHAPTER 5

DEFENSIVE Strategies

Half of soccer is offense: moving the ball down the field and attempting to score in the opponent's goal. The other critical half is defense. A soccer team must have a strong defense to keep the opposing team from scoring in their goal. It is not enough just to have a strong goalkeeper: A goalkeeper, no matter how good, is just one person. Against a team of 11 opponents, a single person is no game. It is important that a successful team has a strong defense as a whole, where each defensive player can effectively work together to mount a strong overall defense.

When a penalty is taken, defenders will mark the offensive players who might be able to get the ball and shoot on the goal.

MARKING

As in many team sports, part of defensive strategy in soccer is watching the other team. A team will easily score a goal if one of its offensive players can get into an open position with a shot at the goal. Then, it is just a matter of someone passing the ball to the open player.

One smart defensive strategy to avoid this is called **marking**. In this strategy, a team's defense makes sure that all of the offensive players on the opposing team are guarded at all times, so that they cannot move into an open position with a clear shot at the goal.

There are a couple types of marking. One often-used type is man-to-man marking, where each defender marks an offensive player. Another frequently used type is zonal marking, where each defender covers a particular area of the soccer field and is tasked with defending against any offensive player who enters that particular zone. In professional soccer leagues, the more commonly used type of marking is zonal, because it tends to be a little more flexible than man-to-man marking. However, some teams will use a combination of zonal marking and man-to-man marking.

Defenders have to stay close to the player they are marking.

When a defensive player tracks an opposing player, they try to visualize where that player is headed.

TRACKING

Another defensive strategy is tracking. This is where the defenders watch the actions and formation of the players on the opposing team, and try to predict where they are heading. For example, a striker could be running to get into position to receive a pass, but they could also be running to distract another defender, so that another forward from the striker's team can move into position to get the ball and score.

Tracking is not an exact science. It is more of an art, and it requires visualization skills. The defender must visualize where their opponent is headed and what the opponent's endgame might be. The defender can then adopt an appropriate defense.

PUSHING TO THE SIDES

Another way to make sure a team's offense does not get a shot at the goal is for the other team to push the player with the ball toward the outer edges of the field. The defenders cannot use their hands to touch the other player, but they can use their body as a kind of shield and guide the offensive player toward the edges of the field. From the edge, it is very difficult for an offensive player to get a good, clear shot at the goal.

Players on the edges still have to be guarded, though. A player at the edge of the field may find it difficult to get a clear shot at the goal, but they can pass to another player who may have a better shot. A strong defense cannot simply push offensive forwards to the side of the field—they must continue to guard their opponents until the ball is back in their position, and they can move it down the field toward the opposing team's goal.

Guarding the ball from an opponent involves both physical skill and mental strategy.

EARLY AND LATE TEAM DEFENSE

To mount an effective defense, teams must agree on their overall defense strategy. In general, there are two types of defense: early and late. Early defense is when a team starts using defense tactics as soon as the opposing team gains control of the ball. Late defense is when a team takes time to recover and regroup after losing control of the ball.

Early defense is useful when an opposing team is particularly skillful at offense. If the opposing team tends to get the ball and quickly and effectively moves it to the goal, then an early defense strategy is probably very wise.

If the opposing team makes a slower, more deliberate move toward the goal, then a late defense might be better. In a late defense, the defenders have generally moved back closer to their goal. This creates fewer gaps in the field through which the ball can be passed by the offensive team. It is a more compact formation of defensive players, and it can be very effective—unless the opposing team is particularly fast at moving the ball into scoring position, in which case, there may not be time to mount a late defense.

It is up to the coach to decide the defensive strategy for the team.

Defenders will do everything in their power to keep the ball from getting near the goalie.

OFFSIDE

If an offensive player who does not have the ball gets too close to the goal, a smart defensive strategy is to trap the offensive player in an offside position. An offensive player may move close to the goal so that a teammate can pass to them for a shot at the goal, but if the defense of the opposing team then moves forward before the player gets the ball, the player is trapped offside. The game play is stopped, and the referee will give the ball to the defense to take a free kick and blast the ball far away from their goal. It is a simple, yet very effective, strategy.

With a strong defense and a fast-moving offense, a team can become a formidable force on the field.

CHAPTER 6

GAME-DAY Ready!

All the practices, drills, and mental exercises are done in preparation for the big game. The coach has spent countless hours working with the players on athletic performance, and the best teams have worked on group mental strategy, too. When the big day comes, whether it is in front of a handful of cheering parents or thousands of screaming fans, players are ready to give it their all.

MENTAL STRATEGIES FOR THE BIG GAME

One way that individual players can prepare for top performance is by using their own mental strategies. Players can choose from a number of methods that will help calm performance nerves and hone their focusing skills.

Preparing the team for the game is every bit as important as prepping individual players.

Follow a Pregame Routine

Patrick Cohn, who writes for a website called Soccer Psychology Tips, says that having a pregame mental warm-up can boost confidence, shake off anxiety, and focus on the game plan. In fact, he compares the mental warm-up to a physical warm-up before a game. If a player started playing a game without first stretching and warming up, they would not play their best, and they might even get injured. The same is true for players who skip a mental warm-up before a game: They will not play their best, and it may hurt their confidence.

Pregame routines can include drills and mental warm-ups.

A person's individual pregame routine can be anything that helps them focus, relax, and boost their confidence. For some people, that may be meditation or prayer. For others, it might be reciting positive affirmations. Whatever it is, Cohn recommends that players develop a pregame routine and stick to it—he considers it as important as a physical warm-up.

Focus on the Game, Not the Competition

Cohn says that soccer players often fall into the trap of comparing themselves to their competitors, which can be damaging to their play. Instead of psyching themselves out by focusing on their competitors' strengths and their own weaknesses, Cohn says players should focus solely on their pregame routine and the game play.

Trust in Your Skills

When players do not trust their own skills, they can start thinking too much during the game. Thinking is great—outside of the game. A player can reflect on their weak spots and areas for improvement in general, and this can be a way to help set small, manageable goals to improve their game. Reflecting on performance and areas for improvement after the game can also be useful—after all, people learn from their mistakes. However, these things should not be dwelled on during the game or in the time immediately before the game starts.

Players should simply trust in their skills right before the game and during play. They should be playing by feel, not focusing on mechanics. The time for focusing on mechanics is during practice and drills. During game time, playing by feel and trusting oneself is the best approach.

Goalies do not have time to think. They must trust in their preparation and skills when the ball comes hurtling toward them.

In rare quiet moments on the soccer field, players can regroup and reset their focus.

Focus on the Process, Not the Results

Focusing on the end results—winning the game—can be damaging. Of course, players want to think positively, but if they focus too much on the end goal, it can actually harm their game play. It is more effective to focus simply on playing the game, and then positive results often occur. If players keep their head in the game and focus on playing strong, a win often follows.

Focus, Focus, Focus

In addition to focusing on the process and not the result, players also need to learn how to focus in general. Focusing is a skill that is important in virtually everything. Students need to be able to focus at school to succeed, and adults need to be able to focus on tasks at their job in order to get paid. Likewise, athletes need to focus on the game to play well.

Sometimes, it can be difficult for an athlete to focus when playing in front of a crowd of fans. Fans can be very distracting, especially when there are thousands of them cheering—or booing. They can be loud and persistent.

The best players will learn to tune out the fans and any other sideline distractions, and focus on the game at hand. They will also learn to set aside any other distractions—tasks they need to accomplish outside of the game, personal problems they may be having, or whatever is troubling their mind. For the duration of the game, strong players will set aside those worries and focus on the game.

Sports psychologists can teach players and coaches different techniques for focusing, including **meditation**, visualization, and **arousal regulation**. With practice, players can use these techniques to improve their focus and effectively drown out the "noise" from outside the game.

Visualize, Visualize, Visualize

Before the big game, players can work on visualizing their game play. They can visualize themselves moving the ball on the field, dribbling, passing to their teammates, scoring goals, or defending against the opposing team. A goalkeeper might visualize blocking goal after goal.

Visualization is a powerful tool for building confidence and skills.

Some athletes find that music is an effective relaxation tool.

There are two types of visualization. In internal visualization, players imagine themselves performing the actions they want to accomplish during the game. Equally useful is external visualization, where players imagine watching themselves performing these actions, as if they are watching a movie. Either method works. Both will help the player accomplish the action automatically, without even really thinking about it. Players will have "practiced" the action in their minds so much that it becomes second nature.

Relax

Relaxation is incredibly important. A tense or anxious player will not play well. It is important for players to learn to relax before a game. For many, using a pregame routine brings about a state of calm readiness. Some players like to listen to certain types of music. Others like to engage in a relaxing activity, such as reading or meditating quietly, alone. Some find prayer relaxing. Whatever method calms a player down, this is what the player should use.

This technique is known as arousal regulation, and it can work in different ways. Players can regulate their arousal to relax themselves, or they can increase their arousal to get "pumped" before a game. Either way, they are using techniques that work well for monitoring and controlling their level of arousal during the game.

Make Goals

This technique does not refer to the actual scoring of goals. Instead, it refers to having players or the team as a whole set small, manageable, achievable goals.

Setting a goal that is too big or unachievable will backfire. If the team or player has no real hope of accomplishing the goal, it will do little other than damage confidence. Appropriate goals can give players and the team something concrete to work toward.

For example, a team at the bottom of its league would not necessarily set a goal of defeating the top team in the league 10-0. However, the team might set a more realistic goal of scoring more goals than it did in the previous game against the winning team. Or, a team that narrowly lost to an opponent in the past might set a goal of winning the rematch.

Whatever the goal is, it should be tough enough to give the players and team something to work toward—but not so tough that they have no hope of accomplishing it.

Good players make goals and look toward them.

Confidence on the field leads to stronger, better play.

Build Confidence

Confidence is critically important on the soccer field. Professional midfielder Filip Prostran feels that building confidence is every bit as important as sharpening athletic skills, such as kicking, dribbling, shooting, and passing. Prostran shared some tips about how to build confidence as a soccer player.

To build confidence, he says, players should try using positive self-talk and affirmations—they should make or write positive statements about themselves daily. They might even try writing these in a soccer journal or a self-confidence letter. Players can also use visualization to picture themselves performing well on the soccer field.

Prostran cautions that these confidence-building strategies do not provide results overnight. It takes time and discipline to keep at these techniques. But players who practice them will ultimately see results.

ALL IN THE MIND

Brain It Like Beckham

In 1998, young soccer star David Beckham was sent off from a World Cup game for kicking another player. Beckham said the kick was a reflex action, because he was in pain and the other player touched him. The referee disagreed and removed Beckham from the game.

The incident turned Beckham from everyone's favorite soccer star into a number one villain. The English team went on to lose the game on a penalty kick, and some said that if Beckham had stayed in the game and taken the kick, England would have won. Beckham was called a "stupid boy" in a newspaper, and people burned his picture. He and his family received death threats.

Beckham thought about giving up soccer, but his manager at Manchester United, Sir Alex Ferguson, encouraged him not to. He told Beckham, "Get yourself back to Manchester to the people that love you, and you'll be fine."

Beckham did just that. He worked on his game, and more importantly, he learned how to manage the psychological stress of being in the spotlight. Beckham went on to have a long and celebrated career and is remembered as one of soccer's greatest stars.

David Beckham learned how to manage the pressure of being an internationally celebrated athlete.

A GAME OF WITS

The rules of soccer are not especially complicated, but it is a fast-moving game with a lot of strategy behind the plays. The best soccer players are fast and athletic, but they also spend time studying the game and other players. They carefully plan positioning and play to help lead their team to win. With practice and the use of mental strategies, players can find themselves at the top of their game.

Soccer: a game of both wits and guts.

GLOSSARY

arousal regulation the ability to regulate one's alertness and performance level

athleticism strength, fitness, and agility in an athlete

bladder an inflated, hollow sack

cocky arrogant or overly bold

dexterity skill in performing tasks

drill intensive practice or training in a particular skill

external imagery imagining oneself as if watching a movie

extrinsically outside of the self

FIFA the acronym for Fédération Internationale de Football Association, the international governing body of soccer

goal setting setting small, manageable goals to achieve an overall greater goal

internal imagery imagining oneself as part of the action

intrinsically inside the self

marking in soccer, guarding an offensive player even when he doesn't have the ball

Medieval Europe Europe between the fifth and fifteenth centuries

meditation to sit quietly and focus completely on one's thoughts or religion

mental agility mental quickness or sharpness

mental state state of mind

mental strength individual toughness or resilience

motivation the reasons one has for acting a certain way

neuroscience the science that studies the functions, abnormalities, and so on of the nervous system

offensive team the team that has the ball and is trying to move toward or score on the goal

offside rule a rule that states that a player is in an offside position if they are nearer to the opponent's goal line than the ball and the second-last opponent. The goalkeeper is considered the last opponent.

predecessor someone who comes before

self-talk words or phrases a person says to themselves to be more effective in reaching a goal

stigma disgrace associated with particular circumstances.

strategy a plan to help one meet a goal

unity a sense of the team working as a whole, rather than as separate, individual players

FOR MORE INFORMATION

BOOKS

Latham, Andrew. *Soccer Smarts for Kids: 60 Skills, Strategies, and Secrets*. Berkeley, CA: Rockridge Press, 2016.

Part, Michael. *Cristiano Ronaldo: The Rise of a Winner*. Beverly Hills, CA: Sole Books, 2014.

Part, Michael. *The Flea: The Amazing Story of Leo Messi*. Beverly Hills, CA: Sole Books, 2013.

WEBSITES

Find more information on all sports, including soccer, at:
www.brainpop.com/health/sportsandfitness

Discover how soccer works, from equipment and rules to player biographies, at:
www.ducksters.com/sports/soccer.php

This FIFA website explains the game in an easy-to-understand way:
grassroots.fifa.com/en/for-kids.html

Read the online Sports Illustrated especially for younger readers at:
www.sikids.com

Publisher's note to educators and parents: Our editors have carefully reviewed these websites to ensure that they are suitable for students. Many websites change frequently, however, and we cannot guarantee that a site's future contents will continue to meet our high standards of quality and educational value. Be advised that students should be closely supervised whenever they access the Internet.

INDEX

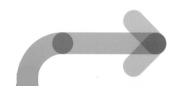

Longwood Jr. High School
198 Longwood Rd.
Middle Island, NY 11953